ADVANCE PRAISE

The Shape of Things to Come, John Blair's deeply considered and deeply felt exploration of the creation of the atomic bomb, takes its epigraph from Ginsberg, and Blair is clearly among Ginsberg's heirs. Blair's research is meticulous, but these poems are more candescence than history; their needle hangs, quivering, in perfect balance between beautiful and awful; their caesuras and fragments constantly disrupt what can be said and understood with the stutters of what never can be. This riveting work brings together the best qualities of both narrative and lyric to illuminate everything, past and present, in the blinding blaze of atomic Moloch, "a sun /...rising too bright to see & burning / hot enough to sear away even this lonely unendurable world."

Catherine Carter, author of *Larvae of the Nearest Stars* and *Marks of the Witch*

In his deeply moving new collection, *The Shape of Things to Come*, John Blair offers us penetrating meditation on the Manhattan Project and its consequences, in terms both historically recuperative and, mindful of a cautionary anxiety, deeply psychological. Here the author borrows from a communal legacy of ancient story to situate the bomb, in spite and in light of its break with the past, as both an illumination of human nature and a shift of mythical scope and weight. In light of the new Zeitgeist and a threat as extreme as ever and yet faded from conversation, this book breathes new life into a much needed public understanding. With lyric ingenuity and grace, it asks us to weigh once more the "sword" hammered by a "three-fissioned God" as one might "words against a future in which every/ prayer is for requital." A profound achievement.

> Bruce Bond, author of twenty-seven books including *Immanent Distance: Poetry and the Metaphysics of the Near at Hand* and *For the Lost Cathedral*

Building upon the achievements of his previous work, *Playful Song Called Beautiful*, John Blair, in *The Shape of Things to Come*, investigates the soul of humanity through the destruction of the 20th century, centering on the Ground Zero of the Trinity test in the Jornada del Muerto desert, "counting down from nothing / at all to everything." It's a tour of history both closely rendered, from a description of a child riding a bus to the voice of a town manager, and large in ambition, where science clothes us "like kings or prophets bearing /wonderful   unspeakable gifts," succeeding wonderfully in both.

> John Gallaher, author of the Levis Poetry Prize–winner *The Little Book of Guesses* and *Map of the Folded World*

ALSO BY JOHN BLAIR

POETRY

Playful Song Called Beautiful
The Green Girls
The Occasions of Paradise

SHORT STORIES

American Standard

NOVELS

A Landscape of Darkness
Bright Angel

THE SHAPE OF THINGS TO COME

POEMS

JOHN BLAIR

ARLINGTON VA

Published by Gival Press, an imprint of Gival Press, LLC.
For information please write:
Gival Press, LLC
P. O. Box 3812
Arlington, VA 22203
www.givalpress.com

First edition
ISBN: 978-1940724-47-8
eISBN: 978-1-940724-48-5

Library of Congress Control Number: 2023942711
Cover art: © Romolo Tavani.
Design by Ken Schellenberg.

Radioactive Nemesis were you there at the beginning
  black dumb tongueless unsmelling blast of Disil-
    lusion?
I manifest your Baptismal Word after four billion years
I guess your birthday in Earthling Night, I salute your
  dreadful presence last majestic as the Gods. . . .
    Allen Ginsberg, "Plutonian Ode"

Out beyond ideas of wrongdoing
and rightdoing there is a field.
I'll meet you there.
When the soul lies down in that grass
the world is too full to talk about.
    Jalāl ad-Dīn Muhammad Rūmī, "A Great Wagon"

CONTENTS

I. THE SHAPE OF THINGS TO COME

The Shape of Things to Come

Szilard stepped off of the curb. As he crossed the street time cracked
open before him and he saw a way to the future, death into the world
and all our woe, the shape of things to come.
  Richard Rhodes, The Making of the Atomic Bomb

It is 1933 and it begins as things
sometimes do   with a drop of rain
     with a man stepping off a curb
deep in some kind of thought
about the nature of divisibility

     mind trained like an unseeing eye
to see   through a wet scrim
of impossible   because reality
is attention   the second look
the world gives us because we dared

look back   and through our givens
     our putatives   our weltanschauung
like the air that we pass through
mid-step   one-footed   between
pavement and cobblestones

a vision comes   divides   here
from now   God from reason
     clean from broken   two
from one   single   pendulous
     drop hung   just barely

from the felted edge of his black
hat's brim   though not
just one drop in and of itself
but one drop becoming two
        an exquisite liquid parting

charged with all the simple art
of mitosis   of fission   his eye's
mind seeing down and deep
        past the misted uncertainty
of electron shells to the innermost

sibylline crux   the kernel
        unbroken and unbloomed
of a nucleus   the shivering
of discontinuity   gelid
in the gloaming   a center

giving way to destiny   to torrents
        to exponential chains
of uncoupled mass   inevitable
as rain falling in its multitudes
        as any moment stretched

to breaking   finally letting go
    to drop like a lie from a lip
like a child   every child
        from grace   a child
every child   one foot hovered

over the stony surface of inevitability
        whose God still calls his name
in the wilderness   whose God
still in all his burning & unreasonable
glory   loves him   just not

enough (as the gate to the garden
swings shut   as the drop drops
and a shoe touches worn leather
to wet and weeping cobblestones)
        to save him.

Seeking Dr. Einstein

> *Szilard leaned his sweaty head out the car window. "Say," he began,*
> *"do you by any chance know where Einstein lives?"*
>   Steve Sheinkin, *Bomb: The Race to Build--and Steal--the*
>   *World's Most Dangerous Weapon*

Even genius has a summer
     hazy perhaps with possibility
but edging toward decoherence
or decadence   towards sunsets
or revelation   war crackling
dark-static on the radio & the town
(Cutchogue   quaint   the sea

just over there   wearing
its paint-peeled skirt of houses)
compelled to whispers and watching
as two men (physicists   both
Hungarian and lost in seaside
Americana)   wander
     their black car bellying

ominous as a u-boat along
the Long Island shore   seeking
Dr. Einstein on his holiday
     to tell him the explosive news
of fission   to persuade him to
persuade a president that the unseeable
is terribly real and terribly coming

right or wrong   us or them
a winter logic in a summer
simmering with anticipation
& though the man himself somewhere
waits   relaxed   pipe in hand
    the world like somebody's oyster
cracking itself open   (safely
    for now   out of sight)

    and a boy walks just ahead
Huck-Finned on the roadside
    contemplative   fishing rod
on his shoulder   to guide them
like Virgil (*one appeared in front*
of my eyes who seemed hoarse
from long silence)   to the great
man's hermitage

    they hang for now suspended
between *sturm und drang*
and the rattling clarities of vocation
    for as long as forever takes
on the verge of turning back
    or of going on just a little farther
balanced exquisitely in the heat
    summer of 1939   radio waves

humming inside their bones
with news that will always be new
    for as far as radiation travels
among the bodies celestial
    where any star might suddenly
flare to mark how they like kings
or prophets   bearing wonderful
    unspeakable gifts   come.

The Boys of Los Alamos

What they see (the boys
of the Los Alamos Ranch School
        most of them sons of Motor City
rust-scale   of steel & gritty
automotive lucre) is a single car
parked at the edge of the plateau
        faces inside   indistinct

through the scrim of falling-wet snow
        just sitting   the car's tailpipe
huffing steam   November 1942
        not quite a year since Pearl Harbor
and the strange thrill
of distant war   and now Nietzsche's
abyss (2nd Period *World Philosophy*

        a tedium made worse by the open
skies outside   the world far away
but waiting) gazing back at them
from the inside of an ominously
black Chrysler Windsor sedan while
they play at lacrosse in the half-frozen
mud of the playing field   (dressed
in shorts and shirts   the cold

being salutary to a boy's constitution)
        the moment meaningless
in itself   without context
        a burden like the day itself
that they won't have to bear for long
        shadows growing long-legged
and sulky among the pines

as the afternoon wears through
to the evening underneath
while the men in the car decide
what they've come to decide
    (*this is the place*   one says
finally   and three days later it is

    the boys   & the school
evicted   to make way for *Site Y*
    site of Infernus   site
of Promethean fire   site
of Leviathan   of Babylon come
to burn the Temple)   but all
the boys see is the car after a time
turning around

    making ruts in the stiff mud
before descending back
into the wilderness that lurks
everywhere the eye can see but here
    in a field full of sweat-
shivering boys   the snow
beginning to paint

the dead grass white   a canvas
made just for secrets
    for an image sketched
in footprints to chart the clouded
sky as it closes over the hardening
    muddy heart   of the coming
new world.

Los Alamos (The Cottonwoods)

The trees grow deep
in the canyon's eroded
throat where the sunlight
sinks first   at the end
of every day and the rain
runs off with a kind

of reluctance   among
the rocks and roots
that cross the stream
like wooden riffles
in a miner's sluice
or the cartilage of a trachea

so that its passing through
becomes a kind of shout
      ecstatic   above
the ordinary trickle-sift
of water though gravel

      or if there is no rain
come June the wind
gathers blizzards
of cottonwood seeds
as they erupt   white spun
      candy-fluff

and pushes them   wildly
combustible into windrows
     piled against rock
ledges   dry brush-lines
    currents doing what
currents do   thoughtlessly

building monuments to entropy
    until the spark
of dry-lightning or some
hiker's flicked cigarette
    and then how fierce the fire

    how calm the trees
smoke rising like an offering
    the canyon beginning
deep in its brushy throat
     to sing.

Oppenheimer On Corsica

A sadist of her kind is an artist in evil, which a wholly wicked person
    could not be. . .
                    Marcel Proust, *À la recherche du temps perdu*

Julius Robert Oppenheimer reads Proust
by lantern-light beside a tent pitched
in the shadow of Monte-Cinto
        twenty-two years old & lunatic

with abstraction   & he has left behind
a literal apple poisoned   like something
in a fairy-tale on the desk of his Cambridge
tutor   & to distract himself

from savage regret he has memorized
a passage from Proust that he will hold
ready his entire life concerning one
Mlle. Vinteuil, who in her fascination

with the amative nature of evil
has asked her lover to spit on a photograph
of her father before she sinks
        intoxicated into the roiling

barbarous waters of a kind of love
in which it was   as Proust writes
so refreshing to sojourn   and when
Oppenheimer crawls into his tent

and tries to sleep   the abstract
flowers of evil return to bloom
and fade inside his head as they
always have, malice becoming shame

becoming guilt sublime and cold
as reason   & he thinks of how
Marcel hid behind a curtain to watch
Mlle. Vinteuil's abject passion

under the gaze   defiled   of her
father's eyes   how drawn to her
debasement he was but how nonetheless
he understood that she had given away

joyfully something human
for something horribly divine
      a sacrifice that Proust understands
in that moment to be the heart of love

which *whatever other names*
one gives to it is the most terrible
and lasting of cruelty   and as
Oppenheimer hikes the island's

trailing spine down to the sea
the air is cool at first   then becomes
saturated with the waspish smell
of salt and sunshine

the atmosphere growing heavier
& more complex as he descends
      sinking into heat and glare
like iron into a sun's dying heart

and just before sunset in the held
crepuscular breath of evening
he stands on the damp sand
at the water's edge and contemplates

the dying world restless in its lingering
        the *artistry of evil* he realizes
just another tide-worn shore against
which the future tirelessly breaks

        barbarous as love   *The smell*
and taste of things remain   Proust
        prophet of the exquisite
and the irredeemable might

have whispered into the sunburnt shell
of his ear in that first last moment
before everything else begins   *like souls*
amid the ruins of everything else.

The Case of the Vanishing Physicists

> *...other people I knew well began to vanish one after the other,*
> *without saying where...*
> Stanislaw Ulam, *Adventures of a Mathematician*

Maybe they went into the desert
    into the ozone and the nothing-
much scent of chalk   a smell
as spare as some sketched-in

afterlife of the mind   that place
where the work is the reward
and the details never matter
so long as the equations balance;

    it is 1942 and the war is so
far away it's almost theoretical
    but when a finite subset of men
with an unknown but substantive

cardinality disappears (in a clowder
a congregation a pride or an exaltation
of wandering shrewdness) the left-
behind brood alone and unwanted

in their cloisters   contemplating
raptures and other unknowable acts
of a three-fissioned God   hovered
galvanic in his currents   and all

they want is to disappear like the sun
into the west   to hammer
like Hephaestus slide-rules into swords
while the unchosen wait   as jealous

and as snake-bitten as Piloctetes
abandoned on the island of Lemnos
by glib & god-loved Odysseus
because of the stench of his wound

and his endless moaning; but of course
the heroes if they live must always
come back (*The hero's burden*
does not end . . . until he returns

full circle to cast his stolen fire
into the darkness of others—so says
Joseph Campbell) alight with the glitter
of consummation   their secrets

like vacation snaps they are all
too eager to share now that it doesn't
much matter even to the dead
whose corpses smolder like offerings

burnt among the ruins (*if ever*
Odysseus burned thighs of sheep
and goats for you covered with thick fat
    grant this prayer that that man

might come back and that a daimon
lead him)   and while the heroes
feast for now   lost but found again
in their ordained places on green

campus quads   in bright lecture halls
among the milling students
of the infinitesimal & the pale shadows
of the unchosen (ringed as they are

by the flaming river Phlegethon
and the triple wailing walls of Tartarus)
      they must walk like all men
their flesh in circles that grow smaller

and smaller until they too finally vanish
      more smoke than substance (matter
into energy into light) under the grand orbits
of a pitiless & atomic night.

II. TRINITY

The Taking of Atomic City

Construction began on Site X [Oak Ridge] in late 1942, the detritus
of rapidly uprooted lives still scattered over the ground . . . books,
photos, shoes, pans, tools, and more lying abandoned in the dust.
　　　Denise Kiernan, *The Girls of Atomic City*

Here is the hope-chest
full of silverfish and some
mamaw's tatty labors sewed
by lamplight　　here some
keepsakes of crying

in the turned-out　　turned-up
　　shovel-heave of leaving
uncles and aunts and sweet
Christian penury　　trickling
down mountainsides

past the dams and the drowned
rivers raging in their catfish
depths　　going to some place
that isn't a place so much
as some brand of mourning

　　good enough maybe
for whatever begin-again
you've got　　out past dry-
rock fences stacked by
the long-dead　　the little

graveyards in the trees
where every rough stone
is marked with *born* and *died*
and every child was *beloved*
    past God's own white

clapboard chapels in their
falling down and their giving in
to war's needful cauldrons
    rendering unto Caesar
what the TVA hadn't already

taken in its electric zeals
    inhuman as foxfire
on rotting tree trunks
    until the taking wasn't
losing any more than dying

was a way out   or a way
back   so many paths
worn to here   and gone
    to springs where frogs
croak their death-wishes

to the toothy night
and the blue clay holds its secrets
in the hexes pressed one atop
the other by the round bottoms
of buckets and the bare feet

of lost children sprung
from the loam like June beetles
    to wander until someone
in the voice of a mother or a father
    or a haunt hung high

on a moonseed vine like a shirt
forgotten on a line   calls
them home   though when
they raise their voices to answer
        the words   like everything else

are so worn through   so
abandoned to the weather
or driven away to some far
and unloved country
        that all anyone might hear

is tree-creak   or some birdsong
warble that sounds for just
a moment like hymnody
        barely loud enough to hear
and no one listening anyway

who might ever in this life
take a moment to care
        voices inconsolable
in the wilderness   first
song and last strung

in sotto voce pearls of longing
        when shall I reach that happy
place O Lord? O when shall
I reach that happy place
        and be forever blessed?

A Message from Town Management

We would have planned it differently too if we had thought of it. . . .
We are at war—Sherman was right.
    Town Manager R. R. O'Meara, *The Oak Ridge Journal*,
    1943

Yes, the mud clings like tar
& no the coal has not been
delivered and yes   in every
case you   the men
and women of the Oak Ridge

Reservation   née the Clinton
Engineer Works   née
the *far-vale*   have suffered
      here where the unwashed
are clap-boarded tight

between the Cumberland
and the Great Smoky mountains
      where long have children
of God just like yourselves
given all in the service

of the blood of the lamb
and of the unnamed dead
who in their sodden graves
grieve you more than you
could ever grieve them

you have suffered
because war is indeed
and ever hell   and the fires
do not light themselves
     but know this:

the good day is coming
     I promise you
and the horizon grows ever
brighter as we   the sons
and gray daughters

of *exceptional news*
are caught up   caught
in   made right   here
where everything that can happen
     will happen   and so

hangs inevitable as rain
and disappointment in the very air
over these veritable mountains
     where falling is a catechism
that the sacred woods

sing breathlessly to themselves
before we doze them down
like any other unplanned thing
that someone   me   you
     must weigh like words

against a future in which every
prayer is for requital   every
hope a violence storming
the ridgelines like a beach
     a wind pushing against

our coming as we hear
like Cadmus a voice (*it is not*
easy to imagine where it
comes from   Ovid tells us
      but it is heard)

coming from the air   from
the stone in the mountains'
fractured ouroboros spine
      (*why gaze   son of Agenor*
at the serpent you have killed?

You too shall be a serpent
to be gazed upon) as we sow
the fields   bountiful
with the serpent's teeth
from which will blessed grow

our burden bound in silver
      bound in steel   bound
in the relentless atoms bound
inside of every relentless thing
      and know you this

my friends and neighbors:
that mud you hate is only us
and we are only it   shadow
and heart fixed inseparable
in obedience

'til glory-come   glory-go
      in the accounting of our days
when we confess the ways
in which we might have
done it *if*—that word

(like any curse) a yoke we bear
in the name of the good that is
always less than we desire
but greater than anything any
of us could ever hope to become.

The Thin Man

On July 17, the difficult decision was made to cease work on the
plutonium gun method -- there would be no «Thin Man.»
F. G. Gosling, *The Manhattan Project*

FADE IN:

EFFECT SHOT:
THE SHADOW OF THE THIN MAN!
The shadow, grotesquely thin,
is cast by one strong light
which reflects itself against
a white cement wall.

ENTER: the first bomb
    the subtle premise they never
finished   the one they called
the *Thin Man*   lean and long
bête noire   of our eager
    & our absolute

but just too liable they feared
to going off a bit too soon
for the kind of glad carnage
the allies had worked
themselves up to make
    (the firestorms of Tokyo
& the guttered bones of Dresden
    blast-shadows   flickered
on the world's white walls)

The important thing   Nick
tells Nora   *is the rhythm*
     a Manhattan you always
shake to fox-trot time
everyone trying for calm
     everyone a friend
with questions and regrets
     a brawl of wind that loves
a party   all the way to the end—

My soul, woman. I give you
three murders and you're still
not satisfied   says Nick
     banter go snap   go spoof
as the world clatters like a reel
toward the credits:

     Nick is closing the door
of their room   as soon as it
snaps shut   they are in each
other's   arms   NICK:
     (smiling . . . but not shy)
I thought you'd never leave.

     They kiss and CUT TO:
BAGGAGE CAR –
PANNING ON PORTER
places the BRIDAL BOUQUET
on top of the crate   turns
     and shuffles
out as porters must   as we are –

FADING OUT: THE END
(off set   off camera   off lights
and childish wonder   off happy
ever after   with bodies
      and justice   done glibly
and well   and sequels on the way
epochs of linen clouds spread
      over hand-painted peaks
of mountains   of bomb-scream
played on slide-whistles
      for a laugh)

      and Nick and Nora lingering
for just another moment   just
another forever of handsome
      and serene in their ducky
gardens   with nothing to do
but smile wan celluloid smiles
      and wait as everyone waits
in black and white

      for applause and resurrection
for curtains drawn whispery velvet
aside   as a theater dims
to darkness   and on the screen
      a lion roars   imperious
as a bomber's brute engines
      coughing   deeply to life
in some far island's breaking
      and technicolor dawn.

The Art of Poison

> *In this connection I think that we should not attempt a plan unless*
> *we can poison food sufficient to kill a half million men...*
>> J. Robert Oppenheimer in a letter to Enrico Fermi
>> concerning the use of radioactive strontium as a poison,
>> 1943

O true apothecary Romeo cries
as the poison (monkshood likely
    or cyanide) burns lovely
and fictional in his veins
    Thy drugs are quick—
though *quick* we know

is half as good as *sure*
and always less than tragic
    because in the art of poison
numbers do sometimes count—
    corpses copious as mushrooms
lumping up from a forest floor

    wicked-witch confections
honeyed in the leaf-mold
    blushing like apples
& leaded like Roman wine
and sweet gasoline   mephitic
even   the whiff of chlorine gas

or lurid isotopes babbling
hypnotic in the imperturbable
waters of a physicist's
barbarous & patriotic mind
    or even love so toxically
careless that it stains a young

man's cheeks with belladonna-
crimson   his lips & tongue
blanched bitter-weed
with *the sin that they have took*
    (*O Romeo, Romeo*
little thief of innocence

all chary in the rosy vines
    declare your killing heart!)
Sin from my lips? young Montague
demurs   *O trespass sweetly*
urged!   The drugs we take
are quick   the ones we give

are quicker   we hold our
lovers' breaths beneath
the deepest sorts of water
until the breathing stops
    passion looped like pretty

ribbon through its own
beginning   the boy cast out
    who always dies   who
pours his draught into
a girlish ear and whispers

O love! O life! Not life,
but love in death!   coy
as a serpent   lucid on a garden
path   who importunes the night
    give me my sin again.

Oppenheimer and Old Lace

At a performance of Arsenic and Old Lace *Robert Oppenheimer*
surprised and delighted the audience [at Los Alamos] by appearing
powdered sepulchrally white with flour as the first of the crowd of
corpses emerging from the cellar in the last act.
          Richard Rhodes, *The Making of the Atomic Bomb*

Even without the powdering
of flour he looked the part
     sallow and stooped
and though first among equals
          pretending to be
equally dead [*For a curtain*
call it is suggested
the twelve elderly gentlemen
file out of the cellar entrance
     stand in a line

across the stage and bow]
     murdered for his own
good by elderly aunts
who served their poisoned
wine in the service
of mercy and a few
good laughs—and it's not
that he was a player
or that death is any sort
of act (of mercy or otherwise)

on which you'd stake
your method or your madness
    just a body playing itself
    breathless and drained
and grinning for the practical
purposes of morale   because
whatever they might mean
    the dead have no lines
and nothing much to say;
they come instead

to reassure us that the end
is near for everyone
    whether in the cyanotic
satori of poisoned wine
or the cool contempt
of a hospital ward   or even
perhaps inside a raw blaze
of energies   all creation
broken from itself & delivered
    like a gift from on high

(from whence   as we know
    all blessings flow) because
nothing is real until it's dead
or even really finished
until it's buried or burned
and after a drink or two
    after a pleasant-enough
denouement   we sleep
our gilded sleep   because
applause is comfort enough

until forgetting takes the stage
to sweep it clean again
of the ash-can rattle of voices
    the aunts whispering murder
in the kitchen while Mortimer
shouts at the telephone *Hello . . .*
Operator? above the chalk-scratch
murmurs of the restless dead
    ungrateful in their cellar
Can you hear my voice? You can?

Are you sure? Well, then
    he announces   hanging up
the phone   as near to truth
as the living can ever get
    I must be here.

The Tower: Minus Six Hours

Alone at the top, calmly reading a book with lightning flashing and
thunder booming and the gadget all set to go, Hornig sat in a lawn
chair with a single light and a telephone.
      William S. Loring, *Birthplace of the Atomic Bomb*

For weeks the days have slid
out and back in   glistered tail
    to glittered mouth
in their snake-ish way
     blazing with desert sun

     the mountains that shoulder
close   incoherent and rambling
& folded into prayer-shapes
     templed hands to guide
the dissembling

     dismembering wind
that unravels like Penelope
every morning's shroud of mist
from the peaks   *insisting*
he thinks (a word more intentional

to his mind than the dry
discretion of *blowing*   though
sometimes during that last
long night while the storms
rage he thinks *winding—*

as in *winding a watch*—
and sometimes *winding down*
    as in *the end of all flesh*
is come before me
    for the earth is filled

with violence through them
    and behold   I will
destroy them   with the earth)
its mindless way through
the wide valley

of the Journada del Muerto
    to finally sing   angelic
in the gaps between the sheets
of corrugated tin & the one
slapping wall of nothing

but canvas that form
    his hermitage one hundred
feet up on a steel tower
    alone with the *gadget*
(five ton globe wrapped in wires

like a spidered planet from
a gothic dream)   and the air
is so damp that even the fragile
scent of evening primrose
is carried   sweetly familiar

    up from the desert floor
heated by the glare of the giant
searchlights focused on the rattling
omphalos   of his perch
    and in the light   apropos

of nothing human   a dog
        disconnected   trots
the sand below the tower   stops
to sniff something   a rock
or scrap of bone bleached

to chalk   a soul abandoned
like a rusted gear from a cattle
tank's wind pump   or maybe
some long-lost baseball batted
away by a boy

        who once lived in the ranch
house nearby   now risen
like a mushroom from its horse-
hide cover   smelling
like a hand too long gone

to smell   & as meaningless
as the mange   like a map
of circumstance   drawn large
on his back   places that are
not his place because

no place ever will be again
        (and though he might long
for it   he is not deceived
        and knows what's coming
which is nothing

        or something that walks
like a man   in nothing's
well-worn shoes) and then
the dog trots out of the light
and is gone   like a stone

dropped down a well
into absence   and the man
in his tower thinks that no one
could have earned forgiveness
enough to make it stay

    not here where the very
air is already molten
with impatience   and he tries
to read   tries to not think
of home or failure

or his colleagues making jokes
about setting the earth's
atmosphere   on fire
    and he feels as completely
other   apart   from his kind

    any kind   as he has ever
in this life felt   the storm
breaking into lightning over
the peaks   sparking restless
at the tug   urgent   of so

much iron and ecstatic potential
    and in that moment
the phone at his feet tries
to ring   a single   inscrutable
    ding of the bell

    but when he picks up
only ghosts whisper   breathlessly

in the drone of the open line
baffled inside the unreachable
distances of forgetting

worn thin by the lathe
of the world's going on without them
     alpha and omega   beginning
and end   first and last and manic
with every regret.

Oppenheimer Scarcely Breathed

He scarcely breathed. He held onto a post to steady himself. For the
last few seconds, he stared directly ahead and then when . . . there
came a tremendous burst of light followed shortly thereafter by the
deep growling roar of the explosion, his face relaxed into an expression
of tremendous relief.
> Brigadier General Thomas F. Farrell, *Memorandum for the*
> *Secretary of War Concerning the Trinity Test of the Atomic*
> *Bomb*

When J. Robert Oppenheimer
was young   at camp
with other boys   he was dragged
from his bed by his bunkmates
to an icehouse   and beaten

    stripped bare   his pubescent
genitalia painted with green
house paint   & then he
was locked naked inside
    among the indifferent

blocks of ice   to shiver
himself empty of his shame
    and of his pity (*the clay*
makes the bowl   Lao Tsu says
    but its emptiness

gives it purpose) inside
that place wherein the worst
or the best has happened
and there is nothing left
to regret;

relief isn't joy   is never joy
        is instead the deep well
beneath the moving current
        the river pooling
in its hollows   thoughtless

as a cyst   or it's the anoxic
zone where crabs crawl in
among the corpses to die
because they've forgotten
to want to breathe

in the uncanny self-absorption
of a silence in which suffering
is devotional   an offering
to the mud from which
they were made

and to which they so promptly
return   *kyrie eléison*
        Christe eléison;
to feel relief is to feel
yourself become *unfilled*

        to return to a zero state
where nothing is begun
        where there is no pain
and anything might still happen
inside the un-rung bell

of possibility   of unknowing
what you can't unknow
 for long (*physicists*
have known sin   Oppenheimer
later lamented   *and this*

is a knowledge which they
cannot lose) where
in the intoxication of completion
 you can for a moment
forget absolved

by the profound calm
of aftermath even as the sky
itself flails turbid
with breaking above you
  over a desert plain

lapsed into its relic self
into earth without form
  and void the face
of the deep itself a single mind
unformed before the first

words are spoken before
we made altars for forgotten
gods who have forgotten us
back to whom we prayed
perhaps (just briefly)

before they fading
  left us to live for whatever
time we have in the light
of the fires that we ourselves
have kindled

  to feel relief perhaps
(just briefly) under a dome
of sky a bowl turned
and emptied of its blue
  and filled again

with bitter dust and falling
    with radiance and omens
and a sun   like any rapture
    just too bright to last
that fades away

like any other god into
the oldest of all redemptions
    an ordinary dawn rising
as it always has   above
the distant and unmoved hills.

Inverting the Elephant

I.

When Ganesha   Lord
of Unities   Guardian
of Gates and of All Mysteries
(and most devotedly
of the labyrinth that begins

atop the dark corridor
of the human spine)
        stood in his mother's door
to bar intruders   Shiva
        his father   cut off

his head for his presumption
and replaced it with the head
of the first creature his servants
could find   which was
of course

an elephant because whatever
else they are   our gods
are stories we tell until they're
over   or strange enough
to love.

II.

It is July 1945 and Otto Frisch
(physicist   late of Vienna
where he was born   and London
and Copenhagen   and now
here inside this moment which

sears like a gasp for breath
in a burning room) watches as all
things become   in this first test
of an atomic bomb   inconsolably
themselves over a desert plain

and as he squints against a blast
of wind that tastes of tastelessness
like boiled water or ozone
from a plasma arc   he sees a god
tear itself atomically whole

black caul and cord and swollen
placenta   out of the dusty body
of the earth and *into the sky* as he later
in his wonder will say *from the ground
with which it remained connected*

*by a lengthening grey stem
of swirling dust, a red-hot elephant
standing balanced on its trunk*
numinous *mysterium tremendum
et fascinans* of the kind we emerged

from the *liquor amnii* looking
to find   in hawk-winged auguries
    or as loving faces emergent
in spilled paint or the shadows
on the walls of bodegas

    or in the seething of energies
pouring up for the first time
from a horizon toothy with mountains
    into the shape of an elephant
serenely balanced on its trunk.

III.

    O bright Lord of Sums
make us two from one   loaves
and fishes   the dead multiplied
in their falling ashes.

    O Shiva confounded
in your filicide   three-bladed
Trishula in your right hand
    all of tri-fold creation

in your left   (the three Kalas
    the three Gunas   the three
surging rivers of the body's
blood and power)   witness your son's

human feet where a neck should be
    turned up to the vaults
of heaven   so that you   Lord
Shiva are amazed   this one

and final time   into a stillness
      from which you will give us
your son Ganesha to guard
      inviolate & inverted   a door

through which we can never
pass   portal to the realms
of mercy and delight from which
all mortals   complicit as we are

in the most wicked of sins are forever
& with greatest love driven   into
the teeth of a pitiless beast
that eats the world.

White Sands

*(July 16th, 1945, 5:42AM Mountain War Time, White Sands, New
Mexico, thirteen minutes after the world's first atomic explosion)*

In first light, the glass
is still falling as a molten
mist   a fog   colored
the thin green of empty
Coca-Cola bottles

    the morning falling
along with it   in narrow
degrees   green as well
    just at the horizon's edge
where the landscape snips

it clean   with a blade
of mountains   and though
no one's close enough to hear it
(the nearest living human
is a technician

    unnamed & unremembered
lying 10,000 yards away
at his station   ordered
to keep his eyes closed
    his head   down

inside a shelter made of concrete
and timber piled over with dirt
    who maybe hears a kind
of crackling in the moment
    before he lifts his head

from his arms   before he
pulls his ear plugs out
        a sound like frost under
a boot   ice night-crusted
on dead grass the way it did

back in Lubbock   or Keokuk
        or in some calm cold
corner of Baltimore
        a hometown sparking in his
lonely marrows where wonder

seethes like seafoam
        like wrack thrown to land's
edge by a spring-tide   busy
with crabs and sea-lice
        climbing eager

through his liquids like
a breaking surf   to line
his rocky strands with the same
soft bottle-green)   even so
there is probably a sound

        but the light
that blazed before daylight
        red through his arm's
flesh   is already gone
        photons screaming

mindlessly into space
where light and time are little
more than background noise
        a fry of abandonment
like gypsum sand blown up

the stoss slopes of pure
white dunes   blown over
mountains   over cities
radiant with compulsion
and terrible disregard

    to fall with a fine
exhausted susurration
    on houses   on beds
and pillows and sleeping children
    who wake to find the grit

caked in the mitered corners
of their eyes   strange
as dread or love or the hard
pale light   of some fading
and childish dream.

III. GROUND ZERO

Report Concerning Monroe Ratliff,
Eleven Years Old

> *"Hot Canyon" still earned its name, with levels of 19mR/hr found*
> *near the Ratliff homestead. . .*
>   William S. Loring, *Birthplace of the Atomic Bomb*

His first thought when he saw the drifting
snowflakes was to put out his tongue
to catch one   like a charm to make
a wish upon   though it was summer

in a desert and the world was torrid
with all the kinds of dying   beyond this
dry-canyon oubliette where there
wasn't even a radio that worked

    where even in 1945 the most
modern thing in the whole goddamned
(he loved the taste of that word
        how corrupt & hammer-rap hard

it was   a clap of spiteful he could
spit like a clove) house was the pink-rose
formica of the *goddamned* kitchen table
    where every day he ate eggs

dropped helter-skelter under every
goddamned shock of thorn brush
and scab of rusty tin left bent
and bleeding rust everywhere he looked

every *goddamned* day-in day-out
leaking boredom like snot   until
that sound right at dawn snatched him
      blinking   from dreams of cold

Coca-Cola and catalog girls   snap
and wail of atoms sundered from themselves
only nineteen short miles away
      (his grandpa's place hidden

in its canyon like a butcher bird's nest
stuffed into a wall-crack)   and he'd
crept outside in first light
      to stand amazed   watching

the west glow through a kind of blizzard
      ashy and serene and settling on every
bent back and head   the livestock
standing in their given places to witness

like the Hebrews the LORD in His tabernacle
      risen in a pillar of cloud gray
as a steer's burnt-slick behind
      and the cattle   struck blind with awe

beginning to wander from tainted water tank
to ash-dusted feed trough   nudged
by a hot wind waving the creosote brush
like semaphore   a message from some

other life   cruel & getting closer
      the not-snow piling in drifts scintillant
with consequence   a sharp-toothed squall
pressing ruin like streaks of meteoric light

from his retinas   a smell like burning flesh
drifting from far away into his boy's dream
of somewhere   anywhere   goddamned
else but here.

In the Tin Factory

> *There, in the tin factory, in the first moment of the atomic age, a*
> *human being was crushed by books.*
> John Hersey, *Hiroshima*

The books themselves are rubble
    abandoned shrines
of moments   rumors and misrule
shouting through doorways

bright as salt   & Miss Sasaki
sits at her desk   her body
held in a calm pretense
    of dutiful

of useful waiting   the way
cherry blossoms wait forever
in a kimono's print
to wither (after the bomb

some of the women
of Hiroshima would wear
flowers until they themselves
withered

    perfect blooms burned
into their skin by a light
so bright it heated the patterns
on their kimonos like the metal

of a branding iron)
    & the shelves in their rigid
orders are made of heavy oak
& painted white (color

of industry   color of empty
    color of death   color
of the serpent-god *Hakuja*
no Myōjin who in the book

of folktales above
Miss Sasaki's head
perpetually strangles
rogue samurai in their sleep)

    and the color makes
Miss Sasaki remember the novel
she has been reading about
the snowy north country

    a young geisha lost
in her poverty
    the handsome traveler
who loves her and leaves

her inevitably behind
how the afternoon moon
paints itself like ardor
    above unbroken fields

of pale buckwheat flowers
as the traveler in his train
    alone   homeward goes
every horizon and rail

    every line tracing
every edge   a separation
of here from there   of past
from whatever consummation

still hovers on the other side
of *now*; it is 8:14   she is
looking at the window
    in a minute she will

look away   thinking
to speak to the girl
at the next desk about
something she can never

    afterwards remember
but before that in the moments
before *after* begins
    she sees through

the tall panes absolutely
nothing   not even sky
or rooftops or any kind
of cloud   only

a featureless waiting-to-be
that fills her not with dread
but with longing   *what do
you call the world?* a priest

at the hydrangea temple
of Ajisai-dera once asked
her father and her father replied
without hesitation   *I am*

the world   I name
the world myself   and now
she thinks *this light*
is the name of the world

before it is written
and the window is its book
     like pages too bright
for words   this day

like any other day
     like any other story
relentless   & forever
about to begin.

The Testimony of Ebb Cade,
Injected Without His Knowledge

WITH PLUTONIUM-239 BY DOCTORS OF THE
MANHATTAN PROJECT

I was a want without much
of a reason   just a need
to eat and feed my own
and for that I suffered

beyond my knowing
or my given consent
      was played and sung
like wrong words to no

particular song   and nobody
singing along   just
trifling-poor Ebb Cade
broken in his bones

      Ebb Cade   who pitched
cement into a power mixer
with a mouth   like a crusted
girlish moue   every single

ticking day   to build
the Oak Ridge Gaseous
Diffusion Plant   spring
of 1945   spring of making

righteous war so far out
in the bible-rattle wilderness
of Tennessee that even the snakes
stayed hid in the deep forgotten

of their secrets
        and I don't know
these things I know because
I wasn't told and when

the hurt kept on
coming   I crawled unseen
        out an unlocked window
and left those white boys

in white coats well-damned
behind and never got
a first word of why or what
        just that ache laid deep

in every marrow of my every
buried bone   fractured
or unfractured   inside
this skin cursed some say

by our angry Lord & God
        a son of Ham who was son
of Noah   son of all
the jubilees   and only dark

enough to bleed my way
into the Oak Ridge Army
Hospital and back out again
        busted like the hickory

of a spade's long handle
        stuck wrong-way
and careless into the churning
stone-beat drum of the mixer

to die eight years later
in a cold dream of sleep
        heavy and half-lived
with isotopes that whispered

angelic fissions   like prayers
or little promises of relentless
conservation   of energy
        of giving and keeping

        of going on long enough
at least   to matter
and I confess   we flew
that car in wild exuberance

        yawing around some
lumbered truck and into
a smashed world of worldly
hurt   spun on a red-dirt road

caught limber between
the blind fold-and-thrust
of Appalachia's long ridges
        locked like the muscles

of a girl's hard thighs
against our pouring hot
and maybe hung a bit over
along its guttered running

as we came to compound
and lay these secret sacrariums
among the bramble and bush
in the arcane back-

of-beyond where no man
comes without warning
without cause   without guilt
to make his unconditional peace

and I admit I am a man
and only a man   washed
in my own spilled blood
and I admit I wept

strong son that I was
like a man divided
from himself for the five
long days they waited to set
my shivered bones   waited

for the slow rivers
of my circulation to salt
and silt their metals down
to where the doctors could

find them   assiduous
as blowflies fingering
their way along the spine
of a roadkill carcass

to tickle their counters
rabid with the inexhaustible
raging of alpha particles
and I confess

that when they pulled
fifteen of my teeth   when
they   feckless & dogged
        unflinching servants

the fissile   rebaptized me
        renamed me in their Book
of Hours   *Human Product – 12*
        I still gave   supine

if unwilling   of myself
to their gazes   to their snake-
eyed admirations of my pith
and wonder

        the sacraments of my savage
pain   and when I turned
    myself finally out   alone
        back into the ravaged

and ravaging mountain moonlight
        into the pine-straw
and turkey-gabble of tall country
        I admit I broke   lucid

and invisibly alight
in the atomic night
        and murder rose in my livid
heart   into my darkest eye

        from the ground
from the black flakes of sky
falling among trees whose sap
rises radiant through phloem

    like history through
the petrified muscle and mass
of a nation and in murder's name
I ran   black and raging

    my flesh a debt of blood
and skin too dark
for any mercy except God's
alone   finally free

and dying slow
    in the first light
of this country's   my country's
     promised new day.

Tickling the Dragon's Tail

> *. . . the Demon Core: a sphere of Plutonium, the core of a nuclear*
> *weapon, made in anticipation of future bombings against the Empire*
> *of Japan.*
>> Tom Britton, "The Demon Core: Tickling the Dragon's
>> Tail"

I.

Start with the core
    with how they made
three bombs but only
dropped two

    Little Boy first & then
three days later like
an ecstasy of dominion
 the Fat Man

    and the third   stoic
in its sundered parts
    lingered in Los Alamos
waiting for a reason

    for the righteous shriek
of supercritical mass
that never came because
 surrender came first

(Hirohito's divine capitulation
      The Jewel Voice Broadcast
August 15th 1945   the god-
emperor of the *Shōwa*

      the *Era of Enlightened
Peace"*   pondering deeply
the general trends of the world")
and among its pieces:

the *demon core*   hot-
pressed *oni* of ever-so-close
but no closer   about
the size of a man's closed fist

(6.2-kilogram subcritical
mass of plutonium-239
in two dull gray hemispheres
electroplated with a nickel's

worth of nickel)   left-over
but not left out   a toy
for boys to play *with*
      tickling the dragon's tail

ever so gently to see just
how close anyone could
possibly come to tragedy's
raw edge   to a river

risen and ravaging a levee's
soft shoulder   to the toothed
serpent that hovers like chaos
inside rain and snow

and the sunless raptures
of drowning.

II.

Then consider the curse
        the flash of blue *aozora*
no tenshi light that was not
in the air itself but instead

glowed within the suddenly
ionized fluid inside a person's eyes
(*Cerenkov Radiation,* the azureous
light that beatifies the depths

of reactor cooling pools) and was
in itself so recklessly beautiful
(*la douleur exquise*) that even
as it killed him   even as he

        horrified   flipped away
the half-sphere of beryllium
that he had carelessly let slip
        Louis Slotin (physicist

        son of Israel & Sonia
lately fled to Winnipeg from
the pogroms of Mother Russia)
saw in the last globular

fruit of his labor a kind
of awakening   a bright
opening into the minds
of strangers

who had stood somehow
beside him all his life but had
never spoken because he was
never really alive enough

to notice them until this
very moment   superposed
as they were like electrons
onto whatever consciousness

manifested itself out of the sum
of interferences   out
of the infinite theoretical
possibilities   of who

he would always from that
moment be   the second victim
of a notional curse (the first
      Haroutune Krikor Daghlian Jr.

had died in agony nine short
months earlier   shot through
with the same demonic light
from the same demonic core)

of causality locked cat-like
inside a simple metallic mass
of potential   a man who
for one moment and forever

became the sublime and entire
alpha and omega of original sin
    that same blood curse
of knowing for which we all

were cast out so long ago
from the obscure gardens
of our humility.

III.

And now (though it happened
so long ago)   consider
the demon Kurohime (*oni*
of the bells   *oni*

of the river and of all
the scorned and forsaken)
    her face and scale-less
skin luminescent with all

the clarity of ice forming
on still water   of ice held
close by tree roots knuckling
a river's muddy bank

    and she is as we might
imagine her   so small
    so powerless   and the river
she stands beside   sighing

its slow way to the sea
  is as indifferent to her bitter
losses as the man who has left
her behind just a woman

  just abandoned standing
alone the air (impossibly still
  her breath steaming latent)
so cold as she watches the ferry

cross the river and it is not
until she steps one slippered foot
wholly into the numbing current
that she understands the flicker

of potentiality within her every
aching cell understands that
in her human heart and sorrow
a serpent lives a seed

of fire and wings abiding
inside her the way a sun abides
inside each star pricked
like a livid *irezumi*

onto the skin of the night's
bowed back and she goes
deeply into the river then
  so that the dragon blooms

bright lotus from her twisting
bones, tail and teeth the water
boiling luminescent with the pale
blue light of intention

and in his terror   through
the caustic rage of fog that laps
the far shore her lover (his name
is Anchin   a young priest

faithless and wandering
in his passions) flees to the temple
of Dōjōji and hides himself inside
the brassy gorge of the temple's

bonshō bell   and when
the temple shudders like a boat
in its timbers with the divine wind
of her coming   he hovers

there like a held breath   for one
moment and forever suspended
in uncertainty   in a metallic
humming of duality

of spirit and intimation
        of causation alive in whispers
& in the susurration of scales
on the cold stone floor

causing the shape of the bell
to take on somehow the shape
of the man   the shape of what
he brought into this life

and what he will carry
painfully away.

IV.

And then   finally   consider
the three quick taps she makes
on the shoulder of the bell
with the spade of her tail

      how she hears within
the brass hollow the sound
of *him*   the sound of the shape
of *him*   the way a peasant

thumps a melon in a field
to know its heart   how she smells
the scent of agarwood incense
and sulfur, the smell of fear

      the smell of the river water
on the pavements and the flames
growing hotter in the pit
of her own cavernous belly

      how Anchin draws his last
breath and screams a single long
note of being and dissolution
      of awakening to the voices

that were always there   though
he'd never heard them before
      to faces ruddy with the beguiling
light that bronze makes

as it begins to soften and glow
      strangers   lovers and demons
who say his name in a chorus
of incantation and devotion

      a chorus of all the ten-thousand
possible expiations any man might
make for the curses he himself
has brought down   whispers

sizzling without pity inside
a sudden bloom of light so bright
that it burns itself in shadows
on the walls of memory

      crackling the atomic air like sins
that nothing in this fallen world
can forgive.

Big Bertha

To Texas. . ./ To sing first, (to the tap of the war-drum, if need be,)/
The idea of all—
　　　Walt Whitman, "From Paumanok Starting I Fly Like A
　　　Bird"

In Chicago they had
the biggest drum
　　(the biggest drum
O the biggest drum
the biggest goddamn drum)

　　eight feet of the round
sound of pound　　wood
and steel and the broadest
raw steerhides the Chicago
Stockyards could slaughter up

to make a thump so low
in its frequencies that faraway
mountains just might sing it
　　moaning back like whales;
passions do not come slowly

　　they bound　　they pounce
　　they drum on the skins
of animals peeled like apples
in one unbroken piece
　　and for years mud-city

cheered   still windy with cow-
fire   at every football game
      (*Themistocles Thucydides*
the Peloponnesian War
      X squared   Y squared

H_2SO_4 Who for?   What for?
Who we gonna yell for?
      GO MAROONS!)
until it stopped in the name
of physics and of the fields

      (open & grassy & unmown)
of the mind   & the drum
was put away   stored beneath
the bleachers of the West Stand
of Stagg Field

      next to an abandoned
squash court in which a secret
would be made (2nd of December
1942   45,000 ultra-pure
graphite blocks   5.4 short tons

of uranium   45 short tons
of uranium oxide powder
      all in a pile   Enrico Fermi's
first atomic reactor   glorious
black layer-cake

of chain-firing neutrons
and gritty bricks of pencil lead)
and the drum   the drum
      the motionless thundering drum
sat in its ticklish coat

of radioactive dust for thirteen more
dreamless years   until an oil
tycoon from Texas bought it
for a buck   a single
American green-backed dollar

    and brought it hot and ticking
home where even now it leads
the Longhorn band onto the lone-
starred fields of battle (*The Eyes
of Texas are upon you*

    All the livelong day
The Eyes of Texas are upon you
    You cannot get away)
war-song   heart-skin drum
yawp   impassioned

the crowd rising to its feet
in exponential fevers of team-love
    home-love   self-love
the stadium thumping back
the pure photonic heat

of the floodlights   as waves
of power and joy and zealous
    terrifying anthems of light
break above the field
    (open & grassy

& swarmed like the plain
of Marathon   with heroes)
    beaten in drumfire to shake
the fragile idea of all
for ten-thousand burning years.

On Visiting the First Ground Zero

It was the tower itself
they named *Zero*   the one
from which they hung the *Gadget*
        a galvanized steel frame
with a tin shed at the top

and its foot anchored   deep
into concrete   under the desert
hardpan   becoming first
and then forever   *ground zero*
        because the foot of anything

is an absence   an opening
from which light begins whatever
journey it might make from inside
a cast shadow   and since
zero itself is always fat

with omission   it is
therefore itself the void
into which light erupts
from the first words a god
        any god   might say

to itself out loud when
counting down from nothing
at all to everything   one
unuttered & imaginary second
at a time.

The Trinity Site, White Sands Missile Base, March 2020

The Flowers of Shukkei-En

A child's head knocks
    knocks   like a knuckle
against the wooden back
of a bench seat in the back
of a bus

    his mind deep in that state
of knowing nothing   nothing
at all   that only children
can know before the world
crawls in one ear

and out no other
    and something   something
is still coming   is still here
    in the near distance
so that the hot pressure

of it fills every crease
and crevice   to dissolve
like sugar into our inks
something   something
    still waiting in the high

desert clouds   after all these
dry years   the air scrub-
brushed and sand-worn
and smelling somehow
    even now   of boiling

exponential fission   of so
many beginnings   of so
many ends   and the bus stops
in front of a house   an old
homestead two miles

from ground zero   sun-blasted
adobe   flaking its plaster
in a wind that between
these mountains never   ever
stops blowing against these children

of monsters   who are just
children   just monsters
    just waiting for the ride to end
the door   to squeal its wide
wings open in the angel-snow

of static   of falling into line
and down the steps and out
    and the house   just a house
just empty   and the kid
from the bus bangs through

converting boredom into momentum
into energy released   thoughtless
    as sunlight   as the haze
rubbed like sea fret onto the low
mountains to the east

by an absent hand   and he
caroms off the table where the *pit*
was assembled   (half-spheres
of solid hot-pressed plutonium-
gallium alloy electroplated

with silver and then   gently
      ecstatically   slicked
with gold leaf and then cupped
like hands   softly   almost
      ceremoniously   around

the urchin of the neutron initiator
      nestled with exquisite   O God
exquisite   care   inside
      the way a bird might lay
its shivered egg into a woven-

grass bower)   bumping hard
into furniture rough and purpose-
made by dead Army carpenters
      heedless in his fast-flung way
into another room   because he has

no time for this   no time for us
      no time for sins   salted
like a universe of stars that he owns
no less   than anyone   no time
for the ticking of radioisotopes

afloat in the streams of his timeless
blood   no time for the dead
who wander nostalgically among us
contemplative as particles floated
in bright silver   bright silk

against the window-pane   sunlight
cracking like sails   like sudden
wind in this wilderness   of good
intentions   of fire struck
infinitesimal from a blur

of shadows   from the love
of unlovable atomicity   brushing
like a hand through some kid's wild
hair like a fresh & sourceless breath
      the same wind that blows

half-lived through the oleanders
of Hiroshima's Shukkei-en garden
      stirring the blooms   each one
sweetly poisonous   and bright as bone
under a newly risen sun.

The Trinity Site, White Sands, New Mexico, October 2017

The Different Country

> *The atomic bomb made the prospect of future war unendurable. It has*
> *led us up those last few steps to the mountain pass; and beyond there is*
> *a different country.*
>
>   J. Robert Oppenheimer, Commencement address (1946)

This high   it's the air itself that does
the polishing   the keen whistle
of restlessness   rubbing the edges
bright above this first republic
beyond unendurable

where grows the tallest rainbow
      the most efficient sky   the brightest
 burning sun   and the steps behind us
are nothing   came from nothing
      mean less than the wind

or the weather or the cold raking
fingers that emerge from behind
whatever carven door holds the secrets
safe inside the Cave of Knowing
(not a box   not an apple hung

      mealy on some golden bough
but a cavern deep with echoes
      lit by electric arcs)   and in
the wide valley   is the different
country   blue heaven

of impossible Promethean fires
        humble in their ranks and orders
and ready to serve   and in our hands
the brassy keys (*whatsoever thou
shalt bind on earth shall be bound*

*in heaven   and whatsoever thou
shalt loose on earth shall be loosed
in heaven*) to open the guiltless
bounties of paradise   though this high
        after night has fallen

over the mountains   over the cities
        the different country glitters
with starry promises so far away
they seem unreal and hopelessly cruel
(*and Lot dwelled in the cities*

*of the plain   and pitched his tent
toward Sodom*)   though no less
beautiful in the way that everything
that glitters is beautiful   even if
the streets aren't really gold

        and the places set for us (*in my
Father's house are many mansions*)
recede into an insubstantiality
that takes lifetimes to become
complete   as the lights

        imagined   apocryphal   blink
one by one out   down to the last
candle burning in a window
in that different   faraway country
that someone   leaning in

close enough to make a shadow
    blows carefully out like a *coup*
de grâce on one last life so as to share
    as the forgotten do deep in the halls
of sleep (guarded   according

to Publius Papinius Statius   by
the shade of *Quies* and the dull attentions
of *Oblivio*) the one darkness that is
the same and only country
to which we will ever belong.

ACKNOWLEDGEMENTS

Poems in this collection were published in the following magazines/journals:

"The Testimony of Ebb Cade" *The Bennington Review*
"The Art of Poison" *The Comstock Review*
"Tickling the Dragon's Tale" *Cutbank*
"The Boys of Los Alamos" *Epoch*
"The Cottonwoods" *Epoch*
"Oppenheimer Scarcely Breathed" *The Madison Review*
"The Flowers of Shukkei-en" (as "The Bus") *Mid-American Review*
"The Tower Minus Six Hours" *Naugatuck River Review*
"Inverting the Elephant" *New Letters*
"In the Tin Factory" *Nimrod.*
"Seeking Dr. Einstein" *Nimrod*
"Big Bertha" *North Dakota Quarterly*
"The Shape of Things to Come" *The Ocotillo Review*
"White Sands" *Prime Number Magazine*
"Thin Man" *Sow's Ear Poetry Review*
"Oppenheimer and Old Lace" *Spoon River Poetry Review*
"The Taking of Atomic City" *The Worcester Review*
"Oppenheimer on Corsica," "The Different Country," "In the Tin Factory," "The Thin Man," "White Sands," "The Tower: Minus Six Hours" *ArLiJo*

ABOUT THE AUTHOR

John Blair has published six books, most recently *Playful Song Called Beautiful* (University of Iowa Press, 2016) as well as poems & stories in *The Colorado Review*, *Poetry*, *The Sewanee Review*, *The Antioch Review*, *New Letters*, and elsewhere.

POETRY FROM GIVAL PRESS

Abandoned Earth by Linwood D. Rumney

Adama: Poème / Adama: Poem by Céline Zins with English translation by Peter Schulman

Architects of the Imaginary / Los arquitectos de lo imaginario by Marta López-Luaces with English translation by G. J. Racz

Arlington Poets in Solidarity with Ukraine edited by Robert L. Giron

Bones Washed in Wine: Flint Shards from Sussex and Bliss by Jeff Mann

Box of Blue Horses by Lisa Graley

Canciones para una sola cuerda / Songs for a Single String by Jesús Gardea with English translation by Robert L. Giron

Dervish by Gerard Wozek

Disputed Site: poems by Kate Monaghan

The Great Canopy by Paula Goldman

Grip by Yvette Neisser Moreno

Haint by Teri Ellen Cross Davis

Honey by Richard Carr

Let Orpheus Take Your Hand by George Klawitter

Leave Smoke by Jeff Walt

Metamorphosis of the Serpent God by Robert L. Giron

Meteor by C. M. Mayo

The Miracle Machine by Matthew Pennock

Museum of False Starts by Chip Livingston

The Nature Sonnets by Jill Williams

On the Altar of Greece by Donna J. Gelagotis Lee

On the Tongue by Jeff Mann

The Origin of the Milky Way by Barbara Louise Ungar

Poetic Voices Without Borders edited by Robert L. Giron

Poetic Voices Without Borders 2 edited by Robert L. Giron

Prosody in England and Elsewhere: A Comparative Approach by Leonardo Malcovati

Protection by Gregg Shapiro

Psaltery and Serpentines by Cecilia Martínez-Gil

Refugee by Vladimir Levchev

Sweet to Burn by Beverly Burch

The Shape of Things to Come: poems by John Blair

The Silent Art by Clifford Bernier

Some Wonder by Eric Nelson

Songs for the Spirit by Robert L. Giron

Songs for the Spirit / Canciones para el espíritu by Robert L. Giron with Spanish translation by Javier Prieto Martínez

Tickets for a Closing Play by Janet I. Buck

Twelve: Sonnets for the Zodiac by John Gosslee

Voyeur by Rich Murphy

We Deserve the Gods We Ask For by Seth Brady Tucker

Where a Poet Ought Not / Où c'qui faut pas by G. Tod Slone

For a complete list of Gival Press titles, visit: *www.givalpress.com*

Books available from Ingram, Brodart, Follett, your favorite
    bookstore, on-line booksellers, or directly from Gival Press.

Gival Press, LLC
PO Box 3812
Arlington, VA 22203
givalpress@yahoo.com
703.351.0079

www.ingramcontent.com/pod-product-compliance
Lightning Source LLC
Chambersburg PA
CBHW020211090426
42734CB00008B/1013